The Wizard Of Gauze

And Other Gags For Kids

Compiled by Charles Keller
Illustrated by Ken Mahood

Prentice-Hall, Inc.
Englewood Cliffs, N.J.

Copyright © 1979 by Charles Keller
Illustrations Copyright © 1979 by Ken Mahood
All rights reserved. No part of this book may be reproduced in any form or by any means, except for the inclusion of brief quotations in a review, without permission in writing from the publisher.
Printed in the United States of America   J
Prentice-Hall International, Inc., London
Prentice-Hall of Australia, Pty. Ltd., North Sydney
Prentice-Hall of Canada, Ltd., Toronto
Prentice-Hall of India Private Ltd., New Delhi
Prentice-Hall of Japan, Inc., Tokyo
Prentice-Hall of Southeast Asia Pte. Ltd., Singapore
Whitehall Books Limited, Wellington, New Zealand
1 2 3 4 5 6 7 8 9 10

Library of Congress Cataloging in Publication Data
Keller, Charles.
  The Wizard of Gauze.
  SUMMARY: Presents a collection of jokes such as "Did you hear about... The boy who had Egyptian flu and gave it to his mummy?"
  1. Wit and humor, Juvenile. 2. American wit and humor. [1. Jokes] I. Mahood, Kenneth, 1930- II. Title.
PN6163.K47   818'.5'407   79-15105
ISNB 0-13-961615-2

14756

To Nicey and Herk

Did you hear about:
the guy who went to a butcher shop and asked for a pound of karate chops.

Did you hear about:
the boy who ran away with the circus but they made him bring it back.

Did you hear about:
the chemist who fell into acid and got absorbed in his work.

Did you hear about:
the smart flea that saved up and bought his own dog.

Did you hear about:
the absent-minded cow who gave milk of amnesia.

Did you hear about:
the person who went to the doctor and didn't live to regret it.

Did you hear about:
the baby owl who didn't give a hoot about anything.

Did you hear about:
the person who was run over by a steamroller
and was put in the hospital in rooms 25 to 30.

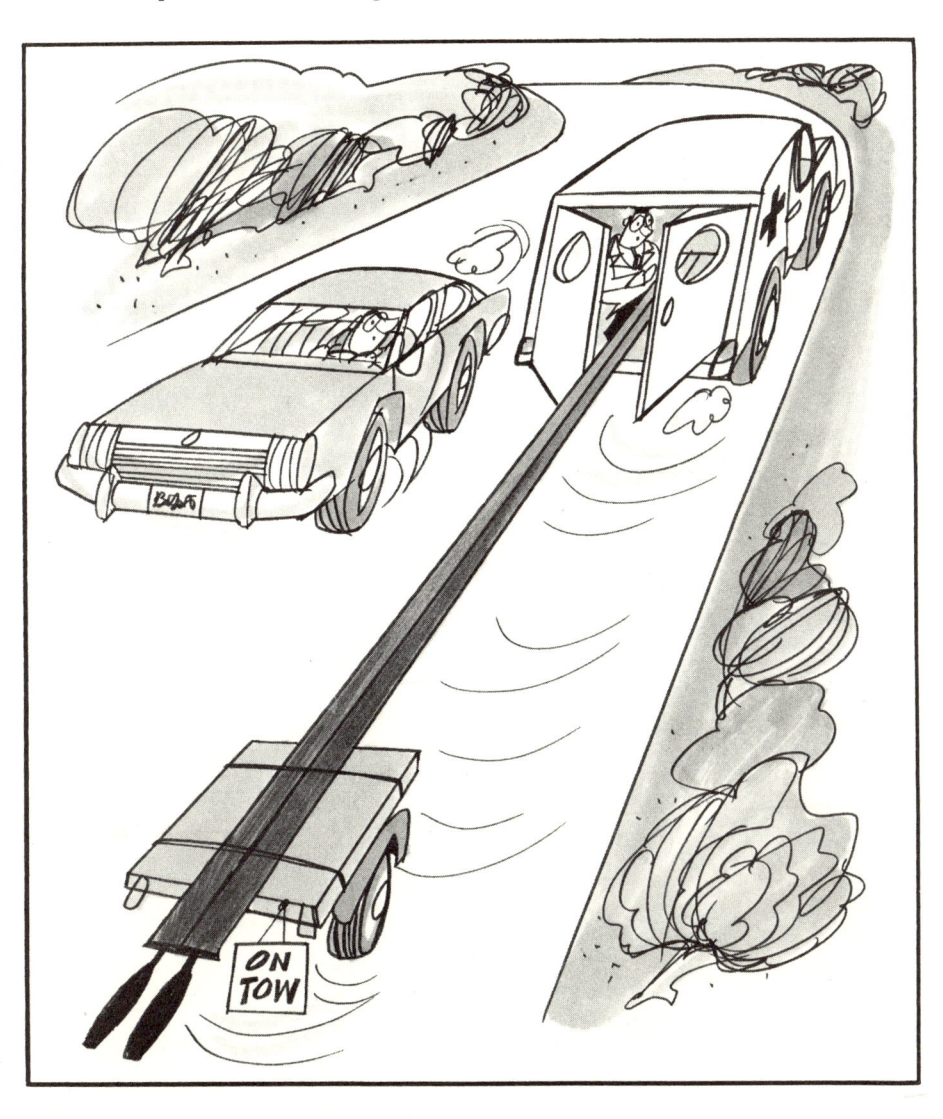

Did you hear about:
the person who always looked at the bright side of things and got sore eyes.

Did you hear about:
the short-tempered doctor who lost his patients.

Did you hear about:
the geologist who had rocks in his head.

Did you hear about:
the person who thought Sherlock Holmes was a housing development.

Did you hear about:
the father who fainted when his teenage son asked for the keys to the garage and came out with the lawnmower.

Did you hear about:
the new car that is so good it runs off the fumes of other cars.

Did you hear about:
the person who thought the Red Sea was parted by a sea-saw.

Did you hear about:
the person who went ice fishing and brought back fifty pounds.

Did you hear about:
the guy who tried to swim the Atlantic Ocean; he swam halfway across and decided he couldn't make it, so he swam back.

Did you hear about:
the person who said "Backwards always are thoughts my."

Did you hear about:
the person who kept both feet on the ground
and had trouble getting his pants on.

Did you hear about:
the girl who had so many cavities in her teeth
she spoke with an echo.

Did you hear about:
the guy who fell into a lens-grinding machine and made a spectacle of himself.

Did you hear about:
the girl who crossed a kangaroo and a mink so she could have a fur coat with pockets.

Did you hear about:
the duck that flew upside down and
quacked up.

Did you hear about:
the person who got kicked out of the submarine service because he tried to sleep with the windows open.

Did you hear about:
the guy who moved his house back five feet to take up the slack in his clothes line.

Did you hear about:
the man who kept his nose to the grindstone and got a flat nose.

Did you hear about:
the guy who read a poster in the post office,
"*Man wanted for robbery in New York*"
and applied for the job.

Did you hear about:
the person who heard a good joke and was going to take it home but decided that would be carrying a joke too far.

Did you hear about:
the guy who broke his drum open to see what made it work.

Did you hear about:
the golfer who wore two pairs of pants in case
he got a hole-in-one.

Did you hear about:
the pigeon who walked around people-toed.

Did you hear about:
the near-sighted turtle who fell in love with the Army helmet.

Did you hear about:
the person who hijacked a submarine and demanded a half-a-million dollars and a parachute.

Did you hear about:
the sailor who, as his ship sank, grabbed a bar
of soap and washed himself ashore.

Did you hear about:
the person who put his ear to a shell and got a busy signal.

Did you hear about:
the person who invented a new kind of
door-knocker and won the no-bell prize.

Did you hear about:
the musician who, when his toupee fell into his trumpet, spent the rest of the day blowing his top.

Did you hear about:
the Australian who got a new boomerang and went crazy trying to throw the old one away.

Did you hear about:
the guy who met a girl in a revolving door and has been going around with her ever since.

Did you hear about:
the person who put his face in a fruit drink
and got a punch in the nose.

Did you hear about:
the person who went horseback riding and felt better off.

Did you hear about:
the person who cut a hole in his umbrella to see if it was raining out.

Did you hear about:
the rich near-sighted man who had a prescription windshield for his car.

Did you hear about:
the guy who thought camels were horses with bucket seats.

Did you hear about:
the octopus which fell in love with a set of bagpipes.

11829

808.87   Keller, Charles
Kel   The Wizard of
         Gauze and other gags
         for kids

Title IV Part B

Project No. 110-303

HUGH MERCER
SCHOOL LIBRARY